THE FIFTEEN MINUTE HAMLET

by Tom Stoppard

SAMUEL FRENCH

ISBN 978-0-573-02506-8

concordtheatricals.co.uk
concordtheatricals.com

FOR AMATEUR PRODUCTION ENQUIRIES

UNITED KINGDOM AND WORLD
EXCLUDING NORTH AMERICA
licensing@concordtheatricals.co.uk
020-7054-7200

Each title is subject to availability from Concord Theatricals, depending upon country of performance.

This work is published by Samuel French, an imprint of Concord Theatricals Ltd.

The Professional Rights in this play are controlled by United Agents LLP, 12-26 Lexington Street, London, W1F OLE.

USE OF COPYRIGHTED MUSIC

USE OF COPYRIGHTED THIRD-PARTY MATERIALS

IMPORTANT BILLING AND CREDIT REQUIREMENTS

THE FIFTEEN MINUTE HAMLET

The first performance of The (Fifteen Minute) Dogg's Troupe Hamlet was on the terraces of the National Theatre, South Bank, London, on Tuesday, August 24th, 1976. Presentation was by Inter-Action Productions, with the following cast of characters:

MARCELLUS, BERNARDO, LAERTES, HORATIO (Scenes One, Three, and encore)	Pat Barlow
FRANCISCO, OSRIC, FORTINBRAS, GRAVEDIGGER, **GHOST, HORATIO** (Scene One)	Paul Filipiak
OPHELIA	Jane Gambier
GERTRUDE	Katina Noble
HAMLET	John Perry
SHAKESPEARE, CLAUDIUS, POLONIUS	Phil Ryder

The play was directed by Ed Berman

The action takes place at a shortened version of Elsinore Castle

PROLOGUE

SHAKESPEARE *enters and bows.*

SHAKESPEARE For this relief, much thanks.
Though I am native here, and to the manner born,
It is a custom more honoured in the breach
Than in the observance

Well.

Something is rotten in the state of Denmark.
To be, or not to be, that is the question.
There are more things in heaven and earth
Than are dreamt of in your philosophy—
There's a divinity that shapes our ends,
Rough hew them how we will.

Though this be madness, yet there is method in it.
I must be cruel, only to be kind;
Hold, as 'twere, the mirror up to nature,
A countenance more in sorrow than in anger.

Lady in audience shouts "Rotten".

The lady doth protest too much.
Cat will mew, and dog will have his day!

He bows again and exits.

Scene One

A castle battlement. Thunder and wind. Two guards,
BERNARDO/MARCELLUS *and* **FRANCISCO/HORATIO** *enter.*

BERNARDO/MARCELLUS Who's there?

FRANCISCO/HORATIO Nay, answer me.

BERNARDO/MARCELLUS Long live the King. Get thee to bed.

FRANCISCO/HORATIO For this relief, much thanks.

BERNARDO/MARCELLUS What, has the thing appeared again tonight?

FRANCISCO/HORATIO Peace, break thee off: look where it comes again. *(He points off left)*

BERNARDO/MARCELLUS Looks it not like the King?

FRANCISCO/HORATIO By heaven, I charge thee speak!

BERNARDO/MARCELLUS *(he points and looks left)* 'Tis here.

FRANCISCO/HORATIO *(he looks centre)* 'Tis there.

BERNARDO/MARCELLUS *(he looks right)* 'Tis gone.

FRANCISCO/HORATIO But look, the morn in russet mantle clad
Walks o'er the dew of yon high eastern hill.

BERNARDO/MARCELLUS Let us impart what we have seen tonight
Unto young Hamlet

They exit.

Scene Two

*A room of state within the castle. A flourish of trumpets
as* **CLAUDIUS** *and* **GERTRUDE** *enter.*

CLAUDIUS Though yet of Hamlet our dear brother's death
The memory be green

HAMLET *enters.*

our sometime sister, now our Queen,
Have we taken to wife.
But now, my cousin Hamlet, and my son—

HAMLET A little more than kin, and less than kind.

CLAUDIUS *and* **GERTRUDE** *exit.*

O that this too solid flesh would melt!
That it should come to this—but two months dead!
So loving to my mother: Frailty, thy name is woman!
Married with mine uncle, my father's brother.
The funeral baked meats did coldly furnish forth
The marriage tables.

HORATIO *rushes on.*

HORATIO My lord, I think I saw him yesternight—
The King, your father—upon the platorm where we watched.

HAMLET 'Tis very strange.

HORATIO Armed, my lord—
A countenance more in sorrow than in anger.

HAMLET My father's spirit in arms? All is not well.
Would the night were come!

HAMLET *and* **HORATIO** *exit to the parapet.*

Scene Three

*The castle battlements at night. There is the noise of
carousing, cannon, fireworks.* **HORATIO** *and* **HAMLET**
appear on the parapet.

HAMLET The King doth wake tonight and takes his rouse.
Though I am native here and to the manner born,
It is a custom more honoured in the breach
Than in observance.

There is the sound of wind.

HORATIO Look, my lord, it comes. *(He points)*

The **GHOST** *enters.*

HAMLET Angels and ministers of grace defend us!
Something is rotten in the state of Denmark!
Alas, poor ghost.

GHOST I am thy father's spirit.
Revenge his foul and most unnatural murder.

HAMLET Murder?

GHOST The serpent that did sting thy father's life
Now wears his crown.

HAMLET O my prophetic soul! Mine uncle?

The **GHOST** *exits.*

(to **HORATIO***)* There are more things in heaven and earth
Than are dreamt of in your philosophy.

HORATIO *exits.*

Hereafter I shall think meet
To put an antic disposition on.
The time is out of joint. O cursed spite
That ever I was born to set it right!

HAMLET *exits.*

Scene Four

A room within the castle. There is a flourish of trumpets,
leading into flute and harpsichord music. **POLONIUS**
enters and immediately **OPHELIA** *rushes on.*

POLONIUS How now, Ophelia, what's the matter?

OPHELIA My lord, as I was sewing in my chamber, Lord
Hamlet with his doublet all unbraced, no hat upon his head,
pale as his shirt, his knees knocking each other, and with
a look so piteous, he comes before me.

POLONIUS Mad for thy love?
I have found the very cause of Hamlet's lunacy.

HAMLET *enters as* **OPHELIA** *exits.*

Look where sadly the poor wretch comes reading.
What do you read, my lord?

HAMLET Words, words, words.

POLONIUS Though this be madness, yet there is method in it.

HAMLET I am but mad north northwest: when the wind is
southerly I know a hawk from a handsaw.

POLONIUS The actors are come hither, my lord.

POLONIUS *exits.*

HAMLET We'll hear a play tomorrow.
I have heard that guilty creatures sitting at a play
Have by the very cunning of the scene
Been struck so to the soul that presently
They have proclaimed their malefactions.
I'll have these players play something
Like the murder of my father before mine uncle.
If he but blench, I know my course.
The play's the thing
Wherein I'll catch the conscience of the King.

Pause.

To be, or not to be *(He puts a dagger to his heart)*

CLAUDIUS *and* **OPHELIA** *enter.*

that is the question.

OPHELIA My Lord—

HAMLET Get thee to a nunnery!

OPHELIA *and* **HAMLET** *exit.*

CLAUDIUS Love? His affections do not that way tend
There's something in his soul.
O'er which his melancholy sits on brood.
He shall with speed to England.

CLAUDIUS *exits.*

Scene Five

A hall within the castle. A flourish of trumpets heralds the entrance of **HAMLET** *and* **OPHELIA, MARCELLUS** *and* **HORATIO,** *who are joking together,* **CLAUDIUS** *and* **GERTRUDE.**

HAMLET *(to imaginary players)* Speak the speech, I pray you, as I pronounced it to you; tripplingly on the tongue. Hold, as 'twere, the mirror up to nature.

Everyone sits to watch the imaginary play. Masque music is heard.

(to **GERTRUDE***)* Madam, how like you the play?

GERTRUDE The lady doth protest too much, methinks.

HAMLET He poisons him in the garden for his estate. You shall see anon how the murderer gets the love of Gonzago's wife.

CLAUDIUS *rises.*

The King rises!

Music stops, hubbub noise starts.

What, frighted with false fire?

CLAUDIUS *exits; re-enters at the side as* **POLONIUS.**

ALL Give o'er the play.

HAMLET Lights! Lights! Lights! I'll take the ghost's word for a thousand pounds!

Exeunt all except **POLONIUS.**

POLONIUS *(standing at side)* He's going to his mother's closet. Behind the arras I'll convey myself to hear the process.

Scene Six

The Queen's apartment. **POLONIUS** *slips behind the arras as it is raised. Lute music is heard.* **HAMLET** *and* **GERTRUDE** *enter.*

HAMLET Now, Mother, what's the matter?

GERTRUDE Hamlet, thou hast thy father much offended.

HAMLET Mother, you have my father much offended. *(He holds her)*

GERTRUDE What wilt thou do? Thou wilt not murder me? Help! Help! Ho!

POLONIUS *(behind the arras)* Help!

HAMLET How now? A rat? *(He stabs* **POLONIUS***)* Dead for a ducat, dead!

GERTRUDE O me, what has thou done?

HAMLET Nay, I know not.

GERTRUDE Alas, he's mad.

HAMLET I must be cruel only to be kind. Good night, Mother.

HAMLET *exits dragging* **POLONIUS**. **GERTRUDE** *exits, sobbing.*

The arras is dropped.

Scene Seven

Another room in the castle. Flourish of trumpets as **CLAUDIUS** *and* **HAMLET** *enter.*

CLAUDIUS Now, Hamlet, where's Polonius?

HAMLET At supper.

CLAUDIUS Hamlet, this deed must send thee hence.
Therefore prepare thyself,
Everything is bent for England.

HAMLET *exits.*

And England, if my love thou holds't at aught,
Thou mayst not coldly set our sov'reign process,
The present death of Hamlet. Do it, England!

CLAUDIUS *exits.*

Interlude

At sea. Sea music.

HAMLET *enters on parapet, swaying as if on a ship's bridge.*

Sea music ends.

HAMLET *exits.*

Scene Eight

Yet another room in the castle. Flourish of trumpets as
CLAUDIUS *and* **LAERTES** *enter.*

LAERTES Where is my father?

CLAUDIUS Dead.

OPHELIA *enters in mad trance, singing.*

Lute music is heard.

OPHELIA They bore him barefaced on the bier,
Hey nonny nonny, hey nonny.
And on his grave rained many a tear...

LAERTES O heat dry up my brains—O kind Sister,

OPHELIA *falls to ground.*

Hads't thou thy wits, and dids't persuade revenge
It could not move thus.

CLAUDIUS And where the offence is, let the great axe fall.

CLAUDIUS *and* **LAERTES** *exit.*

Gravestone rises to hide **OPHELIA.** *A bell tolls four times.*

Scene Nine

A churchyard. A **GRAVEDIGGER** *and* **HAMLET** *enter.*

HAMLET Ere we were two days old at sea, a pirate of very warlike appointment gave us chase. In the grapple I boarded them. On the instant they got clear of our ship; so I alone became their prisoner. They have dealt with me like thieves of mercy.

GRAVEDIGGER What is he that builds stronger than either the mason, the shipwright or the carpenter?

HAMLET A gravemaker. The houses he makes will last till Doomsday.

GRAVEDIGGER *gives skull to* **HAMLET**.

Whose was it?

GRAVEDIGGER This same skull, Sir, was Yorick's skull, the King's jester.

HAMLET Alas, poor Yorick. *(He returns skull to* **GRAVEDIGGER***)* But soft—that is Laertes *(He withdraws to side)*

LAERTES *enters.*

LAERTES What ceremony else?
Lay her in the earth,
And from her fair and unpolluted flesh
May violets spring. I tell thee, churlish priest

CLAUDIUS *and* **GERTRUDE** *enter.*

A ministering angel shall my sister be
When thou liest howling.

HAMLET *(offstage)* What, the fair Ophelia?

LAERTES O treble woe. Hold off the earth awhile,
Till I have caught her once more in my arms.

HAMLET *(re-entering acting area)* What is he whose grief bears such an emphasis?

This is I, Hamlet the Dane!

LAERTES The devil take thy soul.

They grapple.

HAMLET Away thy hand!

CLAUDIUS *and* **GERTRUDE** *pull them apart.*

CLAUDIUS
GERTRUDE } *(together)* Hamlet! Hamlet!

HAMLET I loved Ophelia. What wilt thou do for her?

GERTRUDE O he is mad, Laertes!

CLAUDIUS, GERTRUDE *and* **LAERTES** *exit.*

HAMLET The cat will mew, and dog will have his day!

HAMLET *exits.*

Gravestone is dropped.

Scene Ten

A hall in the castle. A flourish of trumpets as **HAMLET** *enters.*

HAMLET There's a divinity that shapes our ends, rough hew them how we will. But thou would'st not think how ill all's here about my heart. But 'tis no matter. We defy augury. There is a special providence in the fall of a sparrow. If it be now, 'tis not to come; if it be not to come, it will be now; if it be not now yet it will come. The readiness is all.

LAERTES *enters with* **OSRIC** *bearing swords followed by* **CLAUDIUS** *and* **GERTRUDE** *with goblets.*

Come on, Sir!

LAERTES Come, my lord.

Fanfare of trumpets. **LAERTES** *and* **HAMLET** *draw swords and duel.*

HAMLET One.

LAERTES No.

HAMLET Judgement?

OSRIC A hit, a very palapable hit.

CLAUDIUS Stay, give me a drink.
Hamlet, this pearl is thine, here's to thy health.
(he drops a pearl into the goblet) Give him the cup.

GERTRUDE The Queen carouses to thy fortune, Hamlet.

GERTRUDE *takes the cup.*

CLAUDIUS Gertrude, do not drink!

GERTRUDE I will, my lord. *(She drinks)*

LAERTES My lord, I'll hit him now.

HAMLET *and* **LAERTES** *grapple and fight.*

CLAUDIUS Part them, they are incensed.
They bleed on both sides.

OSRIC *and* **CLAUDIUS** *part them.*

OSRIC *exits.*

LAERTES I am justly killed by own treachery. *(He falls)*

GERTRUDE The drink, the drink! I am poisoned! *(She dies)*

HAMLET Treachery! Seek it out.

FORTINBRAS *enters*

LAERTES It is here, Hamlet. Hamlet thou art slain.
Lo, here I lie, never to rise again.
The King, the King's to blame.

HAMLET The point envenomed too?

Then venom to thy work. *(He kills* **CLAUDIUS***)*

LAERTES Exchange forgiveness with me, noble Ha...m... *(He dies)*

HAMLET I follow thee.
I cannot live to hear the news from England.
The rest is silence. *(He dies)*

FORTINBRAS Goodnight sweet prince,
And flights of angels sing thee to thy rest. *(He turns to face away from audience)* Go, bid the soldiers shoot.

Four shots are heard from offstage.

All stand, bow once and exit.

16

Encore

A stagehand enters with a placard bearing the legend "Encore". He parades across the stage and exits. A flourish of trumpets. **CLAUDIUS** *and* **GERTRUDE** *enter.*

CLAUDIUS Our sometimes sister, now our Queen,

    HAMLET *enters.*

have we taken to wife.

HAMLET That it should come to this!

    CLAUDIUS *and* **GERTRUDE** *exit.*

    There is the sound of wind.

    HORATIO *enters.*

HORATIO My lord. I saw him yesternight—
The King, your father.

HAMLET Angels and ministers of grace defend us!

    He exits, running, through rest of speech.

Something is rotten in the state of Denmark.

    GHOST *enters above.*

GHOST I am thy father's spirit.
The serpent that did sting thy father's life.

    HAMLET *enters above.*

Now wears his crown.

HAMLET O my prophetic soul!
Hereafter I shall think meet
To put an antic disposition on.

    They exit.

Short flourish of trumpets.

Polonius enters below, running.

POLONIUS Look where sadly the poor wretch comes.

POLONIUS *exits, running.* **HAMLET** *enters.*

HAMLET I have heard that guilty creatures sitting at a play
Have by the very cunning of the scene been struck.

CLAUDIUS, GERTRUDE, OPHELIA, MARCELLUS *and* **HORATIO** *enter joking.*

All sit to watch the imaginary play.

If he but blench, I know my course

Masque music. **CLAUDIUS** *rises.*

The King rises!

ALL Give o'er the play!

Exeunt all except **GERTRUDE** *and* **HAMLET**.

HAMLET I'll take the ghost's word for a thousand pounds.

POLONIUS *enters and goes behind arras.*

Short flourish of trumpets.

Mother, you have my father much offended.

GERTRUDE Help!

POLONIUS Help, Ho!

HAMLET *(he stabs* **POLONIUS***)* Dead for a ducat, dead!

POLONIUS *falls dead offstage.* **GERTRUDE** *and* **HAMLET** *exit.*

Short flourish of trumpets.

CLAUDIUS *enters followed by* HAMLET.

CLAUDIUS Hamlet, this deed must send thee hence

HAMLET *exits.*

Do it, England.

CLAUDIUS *exits.* OPHELIA *enters and falls on the ground.*

Gravestone rises to hide OPHELIA. *A bell tolls twice.*

GRAVEDIGGER *and* HAMLET *enter.*

HAMLET A pirate gave us a chase. I alone became their prisoner. *(He takes skull from* GRAVEDIGGER*)* Alas poor Yorick—but soft *(He returns skull to* GRAVEDIGGER*)* – This is I, Hamlet the Dane!

GRAVEDIGGER *exits.* LAERTES *enters.*

LAERTES The devil take thy soul!

They grapple, then break.

OSRIC *enters between them with swords. They draw.* CLAUDIUS *and* GERTRUDE *enter with goblets.*

HAMLET Come on, Sir!

LAERTES *and* HAMLET *fight.*

Pause.

OSRIC A hit, a very palapable hit!

CLAUDIUS Give him the cup. Gertrude, do not drink!

GERTRUDE I am poisoned? *(She dies)*

LAERTES Hamlet, thou art slain? *(He dies)*

HAMLET Then venom to thy work! *(He kills* CLAUDIUS*)* The rest is silence. *(He dies)*

Two shots are heard offstage.

Curtain.

PROPS

LIGHTING

SOUND/EFFECTS

Masque music	(Page 17)
Short flourish of trumpets	(Page 17)
Short flourish of trumpets	(Page 17)
A bell tolls twice	(Page 18)
Two shots are heard offstage	(Page 19)

**Other plays by TOM STOPPARD
published and licensed by Samuel French**

Albert's Bridge

Arcadia

Artist Descending a Staircase

The Boundary

Dirty Linen

Dirty Linen and New Found Land

If You're Glad I'll Be Frank

Indian Ink

Night and Day

The Real Inspector Hound

The Real Thing

Rosencrantz and Guildenstern Are Dead

A Separate Peace

**Other plays by TOM STOPPARD
licensed by Samuel French**

ABOUT THE AUTHOR

Tom Stoppard's most recent play, *The Hard Problem*, opened at the National Theatre in 2015. He wrote his first play, *Enter a Free Man*, whilst working as a journalist in Bristol. His plays include *Rosencrantz And Guildenstern Are Dead*, *The Real Inspector Hound*, *After Magritte*, *Jumpers*, *Travesties*, *Every Good Boy Deserves Favour* (a play for actors and orchestra written with André Previn), *Night and Day*, *The Real Thing*, *Hapgood*, *Arcadia*, *Indian Ink*, *The Invention Of Love*, *The Coast Of Utopia*, *Rock'n'Roll*, *Dogg's Our Pett*, *New-Found Land*, *Dogg's Hamlet and Cahoot's Macbeth*. Adaptations include *Tango*, *Undiscovered Country*, *On The Razzle*, *Rough Crossing* and *Dalliance*. Translations include *The Seagull*, *Henry IV*, *Ivanov*, and *The Cherry Orchard*, *The House Of Bernarda Alba* and *Largo Desolato*. He has written eight Evening Standard award-winning plays and five of his plays have won Tony awards.

Radio plays include *Darkside* (set to Pink Floyd's album, *The Dark Side of the Moon*), *On 'Dover Beach'*, *If You're Glad*, *I'll Be Frank*, *Albert's Bridge* (Italia Prize Winner), *M Is For Moon Among Other Things*, *The Dissolution Of Dominic Boot*, *Where Are They Now?*, *Artist Descending A Staircase*, *The Dog It Was That Died* and *In The Native State*.

Television adaptations include *Parades End (BBC/HBO)*, *A Walk On The Water* (from Enter A Free Man), *Three Men In A Boat* and *The Dog It Was That Died*. Original television screenplays include *Another Moon Called Earth*, *A Separate Peace*, *Neutral Ground*, *Teeth* and *Professional Foul*, which won awards from BAFTA, the Broadcasting Press Guild and Squaring The Circle. He adapted his television dramatisation of Jerome K Jerome's *Three Men in a Boat* for BBC Radio.

Screenplays include *Anna Karenina*, *Despair*, *The Romantic Englishwoman*, *The Human Factor*, *Brazil*, *Empire Of The Sun*, *The Russia House*, *Billy Bathgate*, *Poodle Springs*, and *Shakespeare In Love* (with Marc Norman), which won him an Academy Award for Best Original Screenplay, a Golden Globe and the Broadcast Film Critics and American Guild Awards for Best Screenplay 1998. He directed and wrote the screenplay for the film of *Rosencrantz and Guildenstern are Dead*, which won the Prix d'Or at the Venice Film Festival 1990 for Best Film.

Tom Stoppard is a CBE and was knighted in 1997.

www.ingramcontent.com/pod-product-compliance
Lightning Source LLC
LaVergne TN
LVHW020119010225
802674LV00003B/467